21 SECRETES OF SELF MOTIVATION

21 SECRETS OF SELF MOTIVATION

Chris Luciano

Cover design by Stress Design
Book design by Ziyi (Bill) Liu

First Printing 2017

ISBN 978-0-692-79451-7

Table of Contents

Introduction

Why Is It So Hard to Stay Motivated?

This question is asked millions of times per day, by men and women around the world. It's the basis of countless books, articles, and seminars. And yet, most people never find a satisfactory answer.

If you doubt this for even a moment, just look around to the people you know in your own life. You undoubtedly have friends, colleagues, and family members who want to lose weight, save money, move up in their careers, or meet other goals. And, they have the physical and mental capacity to do all of those things. More often than not, though, they don't. Why? Because they aren't motivated enough to see their plans through.

Often, this causes people a great deal of shame. They begin to feel as if they are too weak to change, or suffer from some defect of genetics or personality that stops them from being as mentally strong as the high achievers they see on TV, or in the corner office. Our society rewards achievement — both personally and professionally — so to be without it is almost a sign that you aren't doing enough to keep up.

I would argue that most people aren't weak. They aren't less smart, or lacking in talent. Instead, they simply haven't been taught how to understand their own minds, and never learned how to master their motivational strengths. In this way, they're like someone who is trying to swim for the first time, without any lessons, and comparing themselves to Olympians.

Make no mistake: The world's highest achievers are all using proven techniques to get themselves moving and stay in motion. A small handful are almost supernaturally driven, but the vast majority have figured out that it takes a constant effort to get and stay motivated. They rarely share what they know with others, either because they don't understand the secrets to their own success, or because they don't want or need the competition.

In this book, I'm going to pull back the curtain and show you exactly what it takes to find lasting success. Better yet, I'm going to do it without any complicated ideas or buzzwords. You're going to learn what it takes to get started on the path to success, whatever that might look like for you. And, you're going to see how you can stay on that path, and use the small victories you'll learn along the way to develop bigger habits and victories over time.

With that promise out of the way, there are a couple of things you need to know. The first is that the plan I'm going to give you works, and it can be used by anyone who is determined to make a change. But improvements don't happen automatically, or in your sleep. Reading this book is a good step in the right direction, but you're still going to have to follow the steps I outline before you're going to see the right results.

The second thing you have to know is that I approach the topic of motivation a little differently than other authors or experts you might have come across in the past. I don't believe in empty sayings or motivational sound bites. Those can be great on your Facebook feed, but they're not as helpful as actionable advice. That's because, as you'll see, real change starts in your mind. Success isn't a decision; it's a habit. And habits need to be reinforced on a psychological level.

My professional background is as a hypnotist. When people see my shows and speeches, they are often astounded at what I can do with the right subjects or volunteers. I can get grown men and women to sleep instantly on command, forget their own names, and believe they are in a different time or place (for a few examples), all with a few carefully worded suggestions.

Those demonstrations are great fun, but they also help audiences to understand a bigger point: What happens in your mind first will be acted out in reality later. Once you change your thinking, your actions will follow. The minute you begin to understand that principle, it becomes much, much easier to make positive changes in your life. It really is up to you, and you really will act according to the beliefs you hold deep in your mind.

If you're ready to learn what it takes to become motivated in a way that most people can't — and more importantly, to put that knowledge to work in your own life — then let's get started!

One

The One True Secret of Motivation: Your Thoughts Dictate Your Actions

Most people make a distinction between what they think and what they do. It's only natural. "Thinking" seems to happen in your conscious mind, a running mental soundtrack to your life. Doing involves motion and effort. That makes it altogether different… doesn't it?

Obviously, you can think about something without acting on it, but the relationship between your thoughts and your actions is closer than you probably realize. To understand why, just flip things around. You can think about something without taking action, but you can't take a coordinated action without thinking about it first.

There are some things you can do with no thought whatsoever. You probably don't pay attention to your breathing, to chewing, or to the act of sitting in a chair without falling out. Although there is a part of your brain that pays attention to these things, we're not going to worry about that now. Instead, just recognize that any bigger decision has to spring from a conscious thought. You can't take a trip until you decide to book a ticket. You will never spontaneously rise to exercise without coming to the conclusion that it's the smart thing to do. And you won't get dinner delivered until you place an order. These are just simple examples, but you get the point.

What matters here is that the thoughts come first. And, we can go a bit farther and say that the things you think about most are going to affect your actions and feelings more than your other thoughts.

There is a very easy way to prove this is true. Think back to the last time you missed lunch and found yourself feeling very hungry. In that moment, you probably noticed every smell, restaurant, or ad that featured a meal choice. At the same time, your brain filtered out thoughts about the weather, your favorite TV show, or what you were wearing. Your focus shrunk down to the thing that was most important to you at the moment.

The same thing happens on a bigger scale. When you're thinking about moving, you notice houses for sale. When you're falling in love, you pay attention to all the little endearing habits and qualities your partner has. And so on. Our minds can only concentrate on so much at once, and the things they are concentrated on influence our actions to a disproportionate degree. This brings us to a very important idea you have to understand…

Motivated People Are Focused on Their Goals

Knowing that we have limited bandwidths for attention, and that our most persistent thoughts are the ones that drive us into action, the world's most motivated individuals push their thoughts toward the right goals. They make a point of thinking about the things that matter to them most.

That one realization could change your life. Most people waste their time and attention on things they don't truly care about, while never devoting much mental power to the goals and dreams that really matter. If you could train your brain to focus on your goals, you would find your perspective on different situations, and opportunities would evolve almost overnight. Just like the hungry version of yourself notices every burger joint and pizza parlor in sight, the more motivated version of yourself can make you feel as if you're starving for success.

Once that happens, new ideas and realizations seem to come out of the woodwork. Pieces of the puzzle begin to come together naturally, and you start becoming more perceptive. You see things that were always there, but didn't pay attention to in the past.

Many motivational experts place too much emphasis on the law of attraction, in my opinion. They advise their students to make vision boards, write out their goals, and think deeply about what they want. These steps aren't going to be enough to turn a dream into reality without any effort or a proven plan to back them up. However, what they can do is begin tilting your mind in the right direction so you're thinking about opportunities instead of limitations. That's not enough to make you reach your goal, but it's definitely a strong start.

You Can Shape Your Own Thoughts

It's a common misconception that we're not in control of what goes on in our minds. In fact, I think it's safe to say the majority of the people I meet feel as if they have no power over their own thoughts and emotions.

They're partially correct. You can't necessarily control your instant emotional reaction to a new situation or an unexpected event. But you definitely can change the way you think about things, and even condition yourself to shape those first impressions and gut instincts in a positive way.

There are a lot of ways to do that, but the first and most important is just by being mindful and intentional about your thoughts. You want to be aware of what's going on in your mind, and paying attention to what it is about your existing ideas and attitudes that might be either helping you or holding you back.

Your mind is like a muscle. It responds to exercise and training over time. Many of the weaknesses and limitations we have are self-imposed. We think them, and they become true as a result. In a hypnosis show, I can convince someone that they're trapped in an invisible cage. The bars and borders are completely imaginary, of course, but to the hypnotized man or woman they feel as real as anything else they can see or touch. Even if I place a stack of money just outside their reach, they'll be convinced they can't get it. It's a fact in their minds, so it becomes a fact (for them) in the physical world, too.

What I want you to realize is that the same things go on in your brain on a daily basis. Your thoughts are going to drive your actions, so why not shape them to move you toward your goals instead of pulling you away from them?

Two

Willpower and Motivation Are Very Different Things

How many times have you heard some version of the following: "You could achieve that goal you set, if only you had the willpower"? Most of us have been criticized at some point, either by ourselves or others, for lacking the mental strength to carry out a plan or idea.

The reality, though, is that none of us has the willpower to follow through with very much. That's because willpower and motivation are very different things. When you're motivated, you're moving toward something you want. Willpower, on the other hand, involves the denial of a wish or desire. You get motivated to lose weight and feel better; you use willpower to deny yourself a piece of chocolate cake. They're related, but they aren't the same thing.

That's important, because motivation is the key to long-term change. Willpower, when it's relied on too heavily, can lead to a lot of misery and failure. Because this is such a common misunderstanding, I want to touch on a few of the finer points you have to know.

You Only Get So Much Willpower

Using the right strategies, you can get and stay motivated for the rest of your life. Willpower, on the other hand, comes in very limited quantities. You can't count on it to keep you pushing ahead because you'll undoubtedly run out well before you reach any kind of meaningful goal.

This is an easy phenomenon to observe in real life. People make all kinds of big decisions around their birthdays, New Year's, or performance reviews at work. They really want to make some changes. And yet, a few days later they're usually right back to where they were. They had a burst of excitement, but their willpower ran out.

"But what about those super-driven people who stop smoking cold turkey, or turn their lives on a dime?" you might ask. I'll grant you that these kinds of changes do happen. They're rare, but not unheard of. When psychologists examine these situations, though, they almost always discover one of two things. Either there was a powerful and emotional event that preceded the change, making it a strong motivator, or the individual falls into an unusual personality type.

There are some people — luckily or unluckily, depending on how you look at things — who crave discomfort. For them, using willpower to deny themselves something they want actually fills a need that's greater than the habit they had before. And even then, their willpower may be limited to certain areas of their lives, because they might not derive any satisfaction from being dissatisfied in other areas, if you can follow that line of thought.

The bottom line is that most of us are only given a small amount of willpower to work with. We can use it to begin on the path to improvement, but it needs to be quickly reinforced with other motivational strategies if it's going to be a real catalyst for change.

Your Willpower Can Be Weakened

Not only does willpower come in limited quantities, but it turns out we don't always get our full helping each day. There are times when we have lots of it to throw around, and other times when it virtually disappears.

The difference usually has to do with other factors in our lives. For instance, it can be difficult to find mental strength when we aren't feeling at our best physically. Fatigue, hunger, and illness can all make it harder to pull away from old habits and temptations.

Likewise, stress and mental anguish can sap our willpower, as can emotional hurt. Even being forced to think too much or too often can stop us from making significant changes in our lives. Psychologists call this phenomenon "decision fatigue," and it simply means we get tired of thinking about things after a while and tend to go for the easiest option, which is usually an old habit that we're already comfortable with.

Knowing that willpower is limited, and can be weakened by internal and external influences, we need to recognize that maintaining growth and change can be more difficult than simply deciding to do things differently. In fact, our ambition can work against us if we try to do too much, too soon.

Willpower Grows With Time and Practice

Having given you the bad news about willpower, let's turn to the positive. For all the difficulties involved in denying ourselves the things we want (like chocolate cake), it's important to remember that the struggle isn't futile. We can still tilt our thoughts and feelings in the right direction. But, we have to do it in a way that makes sense — by using what we know about our minds to our advantage, rather than simply enduring the pain of stretching our willpower until it breaks.

Your willpower might not be endless, but it is elastic. The more you get used to using it for little things, the easier it becomes to call on it for bigger jobs. After you've passed on that fried appetizer a few times, it gets easier to skip dessert, too.

The other enduring truth here is that being motivated stops you from having to rely on your willpower in the first place. The positive outweighs the negative. If you're driven mentally to rediscover the athletic body you had in high school, you won't have to agonize over the sweets. Instead, you'll just want to feel fit and active more than you'll want an instant sugar fix. The same part of your brain that made it hard for you to resist the temptation when you started takes the impulse away after you get moving.

If you're the kind of person who beats themselves up for not having more willpower, or worse, the kind who encourages others to show a bit more spine when facing their shortcomings, I want you to stop now. Willpower is a starting point for change, not a complete solution. When you realize and accept that, it gets easier to move toward something that actually works.

Three

Why It's So Hard to Make Up Your Mind

In a stage hypnosis show or a corporate keynote, I like to ask volunteers a simple question: "Are you hypnotized right now?" Usually, they say they aren't. A few are convinced they're awake, alert, and in control of their own thoughts… right up until I snap my fingers and tell them to sleep. Then, it quickly becomes apparent they were in a trance even though they didn't know it.

That's a dramatic way to entertain an audience, but there is an important lesson in the exercise, too. Namely, that it's harder to make up your mind than you might imagine. That's especially true if the different parts of your brain are in conflict.

You can think one thing and feel another. When that happens, the feeling is almost certainly going to win out. That's because the stronger part of your mind is the one you pay the least amount of attention to. In order to shed some light on this, I'm going to touch on a bit about how the brain works. Don't worry, though, we aren't going to get into technical terms or complicated concepts — just a simple overview of the way you make decisions, and why it can be tough to resolve your long-term goals and wishes with the shorter-term instincts and urges that compel you to keep your daily habits.

Introducing Your Subconscious Mind

You've probably already heard of the subconscious. If you learned about it through an introductory psychology class, or through pop culture, you might associate it with Freud's concepts of dark urges, or the idea of brainwashing people against their will. Take away those sensationalized notions, though, and it's just a handy way of talking about all of the things your brain does that aren't associated with conscious thinking.

While you're busy deciding whether to have another cup of coffee, or looking at the latest cat video on Facebook, your subconscious makes sure you stay awake, that your heart keeps beating, and that no immediate threats to your personal safety are lurking at the edge of your vision. Those are all big jobs, but they are also ones you can't concentrate on while doing other things. So, your inner mind takes care of them for you automatically.

I could spend an entire volume of books with theories and research surrounding the subconscious, but there are two aspects that matter most for our purposes. The first is that these "hidden" parts of your mind are concerned with survival, and the second is that they do a lot of things automatically. As it turns out, those are important details when it comes to changing habits and behaviors.

Safety, Security, and Your Subconscious

Your subconscious wants to keep you safe, and the easiest way to do that is by clinging to routines, feelings, and situations that have worked out well in the past. For instance, eating chocolate cake gives you a very rewarding experience, so that feels good to your inner mind. Working out involves pain, and a change of routine (if you aren't already doing so regularly), so it feels less safe.

The net result of that dynamic is that your subconscious will resist change. And, because it's concerned with safety, it's the stronger part of your mind. It can literally overrule your conscious brain. Go back to my earlier example: If the conscious mind says you aren't hypnotized, but the subconscious disagrees, you're going to drop to sleep when I snap my fingers. It's an extreme example of the survival instinct at work; your inner mind responds to the reality it accepts, not the one the conscious mind presents it with.

When you understand that you must convince your subconscious to accept a change before it will result in action, it becomes clear why so many people struggle to alter their daily routines for long, and why willpower is so limited. You know you should save more money, go to bed earlier, and hit the gym more often. But the most powerful part of your brain doesn't agree because it feels like you're safer doing what you've always done and avoiding pain. So, it takes your idea and tosses it in the trash, wearing you down with negative urges and emotions until you give in.

Convincing Your Subconscious to Change

Your subconscious might not like change, but it's not immune to it. You can adopt new ideas and habits, but not through the blunt force of willpower. That will get you through a few hours, or even a few days, but not much longer. In order to make a more permanent change, you have to persuade your inner mind to move toward a new normal. Helping people to do that is my expertise, and it can happen in a number of different ways.

One is by appealing to emotion. Your conscious mind might be rational, but your subconscious is all about feelings. It wants joy and excitement, not fear and worry. So, you can learn to associate actions that move you closer to your goals with positive emotional experiences by rewarding yourself after you take a step in the right direction.

Another way to influence your subconscious is with the power of repetition. The more often you see or hear something, the more likely your mind is to accept it as truth. Advertisers know this, of course, and use a barrage of ads to convince you that their product, service, or candidate is superior to all others while appealing to your emotions at the same time.

And finally, you can affect your subconscious through

the process of hypnosis. This can be done formally, in a hypnotherapist's office, or informally through visualization and self-hypnosis.

All of these methods work, and some people might find more success with one technique over another. Personal preferences can also make one pathway to the subconscious preferable to another. However, they work best in combination. If you're serious about putting yourself on an unstoppable motivational plan, you should be helping yourself by appealing to your emotions, using repetition to reinforce your goals, and practicing regular visualization or self-hypnosis.

Changing your mind at the subconscious level takes more work than switching your opinions or learning new information, but it's also more powerful and the benefits are longer lasting.

Four

Using Visualization as a Powerful Tool for Motivation

I'm often asked what the most powerful tool for increasing motivation is. My answer often surprises people, because it's not a set of recordings, an inspirational poster, or even a cup of coffee… it's your own imagination.

When you become good at visualizing, you can imagine a world, or a life, that's different from the one you currently live in. You can literally paint a new reality in your brain. Once that reality becomes a familiar place, your mind will take the next step and start drawing you closer to it. It will begin to subconsciously process connections you didn't see or notice before, bringing them together in a way that draws you ever closer to your goal.

If you doubt this, I invite you to go online and view some videos from my hypnosis shows. What you'll see are men and women who are using their imagination and concentration together in a very interesting way. I'm helping them to narrow their focus, but they're doing the real work. They are creating temporary realities the rest of us don't see or feel. You can do the same, in a less dramatic way but with more significant results.

Setting the Stage for Great Visualization

If you want to use visualization as a way to get more energy and focus, you can begin by preparing yourself and your environment. You'll need to have a specific goal in mind, of course, but you don't need a special room, any expensive equipment, or loose-fitting robes. There isn't anything mystical about this process; it's all about using your focus and concentration to reinforce your conscious dreams on an unconscious level.

You can start by finding a quiet and comfortable place to sit, or even lie down. An office chair, a comfy couch, or the bed you sleep in will do just fine. In fact, you might utilize all of these at different times if you practice visualization a few times a day (which I highly recommend). You just need a spot where you aren't likely to be disturbed, and where you can sit comfortably with your eyes closed and tune out the world around you.

Although it's certainly not a necessity, know that it can be helpful to do a few minutes of visualization at the same time (or times) during the day. As with anything else, being calm and introspective can become a habit. If it stays a part of your normal routine for a while, your brain will adjust and make it easier for you to focus when the right time comes.

How to Use Visualization

In a certain sense, you don't need to be told how to visualize. All of us slip in and out of our imaginations several times a day. However, there is some advice I can give to make it easier for you to relax and get motivated.

The first is to let the stress out of your body so your mind can follow. You might feel like this is next to impossible, especially if you're used to dealing with tense situations, or being on the go all the time. But, by taking a few deep breaths, you'll find that your pulse will naturally slow and your attention will center on the here and now.

Next, you can use proven relaxation techniques to ease up your muscles and joints. One popular way is to imagine you are easing into a hot tub a few inches at a time. As you do, let the corresponding parts of your body — your feet, your legs, your hips, and so on — go absolutely limp and loose. Feel yourself letting go, sinking into your chair or sofa, and enjoying the sense of peace that comes with it.

Once you feel completely relaxed and are breathing slowly, imagine you are in the process of reaching your goal within your mind. See, hear, feel, and taste everything involved. Mentally touch all that's around you, and immerse yourself in the sensation. Take your time and really enjoy the experience. Imagine that you are succeeding, and then that you already have succeeded, and feel how pleasurable the sense of accomplishment is.

Some people find it useful to be guided through this process. There are any number of self-motivational recordings you can listen to that will help you relax, or you can make your own by listening to a loop of yourself describing what it will be like when you finally reach your goal. Whether you use such a tool or not isn't important. All that matters is that you take a moment to let the distracting noise of day-to-day life fade away, and that you feel what it's like to reach your goal in a sensory way. When you do that, your brain will start making the kinds of connections I talked about and guide you more and more steadily in the right direction.

Visualization Is a Habit and a Skill

Although visualization comes naturally to all of us, it is a skill that can get stronger or weaker over time. Most children use their imagination every day, while many adults lose touch with this part of themselves when they get overwhelmed with the practical details of day-to-day life. Don't be dismayed if you have trouble visualizing effectively at first. The more you do it, the better you'll get. And, the easier it will be to shut out errant thoughts and outside distractions.

As I've said, visualization is a basic human skill. It's a feature of the mind that allows us to think about things that don't exist yet and turn them into reality. In fact, the most difficult part of the process is usually getting past your own apprehension. Whether it's referred to as visualization, mindfulness, meditation, or self-hypnosis, lots of people have a fear of quieting their own minds. However, what they should be afraid of is getting so engrossed in everything that's going on around them that they don't use their most effective motivational tool.

Given enough time and practice, visualization will change your mindset. Instead of being aware of your limitations, you'll start thinking of your dreams as things you can achieve because, mentally speaking, you've already achieved them many times in the past. Why not focus your mind on what you really want to achieve, rather than letting it drift from one distraction to the next?

Five

Where Is Your Mental Autopilot Taking You?

You probably make hundreds of decisions every day. Some of them are small, while others can feel quite large. No matter how overwhelmed you feel by the process of constantly choosing, however, you should know that the majority of your life's decisions are made automatically, without any input from your conscious mind.

Don't worry, this isn't the start of a rant about mind control or conspiracy theories. This unknown decision-maker that's shaping your life at every turn is your subconscious mind.

Your subconscious makes small decisions for you because that's an easy way to keep you safe and breathing, and because it frees up the rest of your brain for more complex tasks. If you don't believe me, stop and ask yourself when you last really thought about what brand of soap you use, whether you prefer coffee or tea, the fastest way to get to work, or which sock you should put on first in the morning.

99.9% of the time, we make these "decisions" without any thought, unless there is a reason for us to reconsider our normal routines.

This is a good system, and an unavoidable one, since we don't have the mental bandwidth to think about every decision we have to make every day. But it can also make it easy to fall into bad habits and reinforce them again and again.

You can't change your behavior, your habits, or the results you're getting from any part of your life until you master this "mental autopilot" and point it in the right direction. It's just too easy to keep sabotaging yourself through a host of small decisions that lead you away from your true goals. So how do you reset the GPS and lead yourself to success?

Decide What You're Going to Pay Attention To

Your subconscious carries so much of your mental workload because it has to. If it didn't, you'd be overwhelmed by every bit of stimuli you encountered. Every sound, feeling, and sensation would cause you to stop what you were doing and throw you off in a new direction.

There's only so much of your attention to go around. So, you need to decide where to direct that focus. That usually means focusing on one major goal or change in your life at a time. That's not to say you have to abandon every other idea and pursuit, just that your mind should be tuned to a single result. That way, you can stay focused on it and take advantage of the law of attraction benefits that come with being mindful.

For a quick demonstration of this, do me a favor. Stop whatever you're doing right now and look for anything in your line of sight that has the color red. Take a few moments and find as many as you can. Then, close your eyes and see how many you can recall. Once you've opened your eyes again, notice how many other things you didn't pay attention to that might have been blue or green. What would you have seen if you had focused on those colors instead?

It's up to you to decide where your focus will go, because you can't concentrate on everything. And if you don't choose, your mental autopilot will just take you toward whatever feels easiest and most comfortable at the moment. When that happens, you'll probably start to feel as if you're drifting aimlessly from one fad, inspiration, or unfinished project to the next.

Set the Course Yourself

Once you know where you're headed, you can start to alter the small habits that are going to take you there. When I first introduced the idea of a mental autopilot, it was to show how it can be an obstacle to change. But that's not necessarily a bad thing.

Being set in your habits is only a negative when you have bad habits. When you have a routine that's continually taking you toward your biggest goals and dreams, your autopilot is guiding you toward success without much (if any) conscious input from you. You're simply getting the job done one day at a time.

The only real difference between these two scenarios is which habits are being followed, and why. If you tend to stay up too late and feel groggy in the morning because it's what you've always done, that could be holding you back from making an impact at the office and advancing your career. But if you develop a routine of getting up, going for a jog, and showing up at the office before anyone else feeing energized and ready to take on a new day, that habit is going to pull you toward professional success. They're both habits, and either one can feel natural. One is just more beneficial than the other.

Many people never realize that habits are habits. They are patterns that feel tough to break because they become established over time. You might think getting up early is hard, that you don't have time to meet new people who can help you succeed at work, or that healthy foods don't taste good to you. If you could keep doing each of those things for a month or two, however, you would suddenly discover it felt strange not to do them. It's truly amazing what you can adapt to, given just a bit of time and direction.

Men and women who reach their goals do so by figuring out what's important to them, deciding what habits they need to set (or which parts of their lives they need to let go of), and then putting themselves on the right path. Why shouldn't you do the same?

Six

You Can Drive Yourself Crazy Chasing the Wrong Goals

One of the challenges on the road to success is deciding what that success will look like for you. That should be easy, in theory, but it's a part of the process many people struggle with. It's easy to drive yourself crazy chasing the wrong goals, but that's a more common mistake than you might realize.

Before I get into the reasons it's so easy to aim for the wrong goals, I want to point out just how crucial it is that you direct your efforts in a way that will lead you toward what you really desire deep down. Most people, at any given moment, could write down five or 10 things they want to do or have. But if you ask them follow-up questions, you'll discover that their list is filled with things they think they should want, or that they would enjoy having, but wouldn't actually work to get.

Those aren't really goals, or even worthy of becoming goals. They are simply wishes, or miscellaneous thoughts. Thinking about those kinds of daydreams is fine if you're making a list of what you would get or do if you won the lottery. But when it comes to planning ahead and figuring out what will actually compel you to change your habits, you need to find dreams that you would be thrilled to achieve — those are the kinds of goals that will be emotional enough to catch the attention of your subconscious and help keep you motivated.

Without the right focus, you are very unlikely to reach your goals. And if you do reach them, they won't bring you the satisfaction you were hoping for. Unfortunately, there are a number of factors that can make it tough to zero in on what we actually want from life and should prioritize our efforts on.

No One Else Can Tell You What to Dream Of

One of the primary challenges associated with setting goals has to do with the fact that many of our immediate aims are given to us by other people. We have bosses, parents, spouses, and even children or friends who think they know what we should be striving for. They might even be right. But, unless the drive comes from within, it's hard to build and sustain the kind of motivation it takes to make a real change in your life.

That means you should be wary of targets that other people set for you in a general sense. Remember that you can agree with them, in the same way you can agree with something you read online, and still not be emotionally affected by it. And if you don't feel strongly enough, and if there isn't a passion inside of you to reach the goal, then your willpower is going to give out very quickly and you'll be back where you started.

The only way to truly adopt someone else's goals as your own is to internalize them in a way that's personally meaningful. For example, a salesperson who is given a quota by their boss might think about the dream vacation they could get if they were to meet the quota. They may not be motivated by the thought of earning a certain amount of money for the company, but they could be driven to succeed by dreaming about two weeks spent on white, sandy beaches.

No one else can tell you what to dream of, so don't try to make other people's goals your own. Instead, decide what excites you, and then make a plan to turn it into a reality.

Material Success Isn't Everything

It has been said, various times, that money is the ultimate motivator. It's supposed to be a universal adapter for ambition, in that many of the things we want to have, do, or look forward to in this life have a financial equivalent.

Research in both psychology and behavioral economics has shown time and time again, however, that money is not necessarily the prime motivational tool that most people think it is. While it might drive some people forward, it is actually a poor motivator for others. There are a lot of us who simply prefer free time with our loved ones, unique experiences, or even the joy of a fresh challenge.

If you are in a situation where the rewards that come from your job are financial, then it might make sense to follow the advice I've already given and find a way to personalize your performance targets. Don't let it be about the money; think of what you'll do once you've achieved your goal. Or, simply accept that financial and material rewards aren't your biggest priority. Despite the fact that we put a lot of emphasis on getting the newest, biggest, and best things in the Western world, there are a lot of other ways to enjoy your life.

Chasing money can easily end up being just another way to adopt someone else's goal. That's an easy hole to fall into, but it's not going to lead to real or lasting motivation if that's not in line with your values.

Be Careful When Trying to Motivate Others

Even though my aim is to help individuals who are trying to reach their own personal goals and improve their lives, this seems like a good point to share a strong piece of advice: Remember the information I've just given you when you're trying to incentivize other people.

A lot of business owners and executives struggle to move their personnel into action, and to create real performance gains in their team. They bring in consultants and motivational experts, but find that the effects only last for a short time. That's because pumping people up only gives them a temporary boost of willpower. That's likely to wear off in a day or two.

If you really want your employees or colleagues to do things differently, you're going to have to help them get and stay motivated. And that means appealing to goals that matter to them, not ones you set on their behalf. They may follow you for a while because they want to help, or fear losing their jobs, but you won't get what you're looking for until you reach them on a psychological level.

Chasing the wrong goals always leaves you at a dead end, whether you're trying to improve your own life or looking to inspire change in others.

Seven

How to Find and Set Inspiring Goals

There is a certain irony at work in the modern age. At a time when humans have the vast potential to follow virtually any pursuit or passion that moves them, more and more people are finding that it's difficult to locate their real goal or purpose.

Some of this probably comes down to the burden of choice. Because we have more options available to us than past generations ever did, it's easy to become overwhelmed by the possibilities. At the same time, we are confronted with a nearly endless stream of information and advice. That can make it harder still to cut through the clutter and zero in on what actually matters to us, rather than being persuaded by the latest fad or idea.

However, finding the right goals is the most important step you can take toward finding lasting motivation. You want to set a goal that drags you out of bed in the morning, makes your pulse quicken when you think about reaching it, and keeps you going when things get tough. If it's just a passing thought or fleeting desire, then you're going to have a difficult time moving ahead.

You may already have a significant goal in mind that you'd like to reach. You might have several of them. But if you don't, it's crucial that you start at the beginning and figure out what you most want out of your life right now before moving forward. Luckily, there are some things you can do to get your mind moving in the right direction.

Don't Rush This Process

If you don't have any concrete notions about where you want your plan for goal setting and motivation to take you, don't let it worry you too much. Stress, previous setbacks, and information overload can all work against you. You just need to find a bit of clarity, and you'll never interview a better expert on what will make you happy than you.

With that in mind, don't rush this process. You might want to make some notes, do some research online, and even talk with friends or family members who have known you long enough to offer their insights. You could also begin by thinking about what you don't want, and using those guidelines to narrow things down a little bit.

It might be tempting to jump at the first notion that comes to mind, or set a goal based on someone else's advice, but that would be a mistake. You have to find what drives you, and if it takes you a couple of weeks, months, or years to get there, that's time well spent.

In the meantime, don't forget that you can set small goals for yourself, and achieve them, while moving in the right direction. Rather than aiming for a big target, see if you can hit a small one that you think will lead you closer to happiness or fulfillment. You'll get some practice using proven motivational principles, and you'll be closer to your dream than you are right now.

Be Honest With Yourself

In seminars and workshops, people often discuss their biggest dreams and goals. It's not unusual for some common themes to show up. Many, many people would say that their most pressing and powerful motivator would be to lose weight, make more money, or give up a bad habit. And yet, it's not unusual to find that they haven't ever taken any action to reach these goals, or even done any research to figure out how they might do so.

This isn't meant to be critical of people who have those goals, just to point out that they might be falling into the trap of listing things they think they should want, that other people suggest they should want, or that are fashionable to aspire to. That's well and fine, but very few goals are ever met without a sense of personal passion. You have to really want it if you're going to influence your subconscious mind, change your habits, and find success.

I guess this is my way of saying you should be honest with yourself when deciding what to shoot for. I'm not concerned with what you tell others, or whether your dream is the dream someone else thinks you should have. Instead, I want you to know that the closer your goal is to your heart — and the more strongly you feel about achieving it — the more powerful it's going to be as a personal motivator.

Think Big and Find Your Passion

One of the interesting things you see in my position is that people can actually de-motivate themselves by being too pragmatic. Realism has a place in goal setting, but it comes later, when you're in the process of refining your idea. In the beginning, it's better to think big and work backward.

The reason for this is entirely psychological. Even though the biggest goals might seem less realistic than the smaller ones from the point you're sitting at now, they also have the most emotional appeal. When your conscious and subconscious minds are at odds, it's the subconscious that's going to have its way. So if intellect tells you to go after an idea, but your emotions say otherwise, you're probably not going to move. But if your heart beats for something while your rational thoughts tell you it's going to be difficult to achieve, your inner mind is going to pull you in that direction anyway. Or, it's going to fight back when you try to move in a different direction.

Many of us have huge, untapped passions within ourselves. We have dreams that are so big we are afraid to admit them to ourselves, much less anyone else. Those are the ones worth chasing, and the ones that will push us to change our lives, in little ways at first and bigger ways later. You can always refine your goals to make them workable in the short term, but you can't take something that doesn't inspire you and use it as a permanent motivator.

Eight

How to Find and Set Inspiring Goals

There are two big obstacles standing between most people and the lives they really want to be enjoying. The first is the need to find a goal that's truly motivating to them, and one that will be fulfilling when they achieve it. The second obstacle is finding a way to turn that dream into an actionable plan.

I've learned over the years that most adults tend to think the first step is very easy and the second one is exceedingly difficult. In my opinion, they've usually got it backward. In a world of virtually unlimited choices, deciding what you really want can be harder than it looks. And conversely, once you discover what that is, your mind will start to make connections that tie the pieces together.

You've probably noticed this in your own life at some point. The minute you make a big decision, things just start to break in that direction, or you find that the decision has been reinforced. Sometimes it's good luck, but often it's just a case of our subconscious minds taking more notice of an idea that we've picked up as being important to us on an emotional level.

Still, there are a few steps involved in turning a big dream, no matter how motivating it might be, into a more specific goal or plan. In particular, it helps if you can find the answers to a handful of important questions.

Is the Goal You're Setting for Yourself Realistic?

You have to be careful when assessing how realistic your goal or dream is. That's because aiming too high, or too low, can derail your personal motivation.

Generally speaking, I think it's better to have a very ambitious goal, even if it's difficult to reach. That's going to be motivating on a personal level, and satisfying when you achieve it. And, you can always back your giant dream down into something that's more achievable in the near term if that makes more sense. Rome wasn't built in a day, and you don't have to conquer the whole world all at once.

It's worth pointing out, though, that a goal that's too big or too unrealistic can quickly sap your energy and motivation. When something is so far out of touch with reality that you know it's not going to come together, then stretching to meet it is just going to leave you fatigued and frustrated.

My advice is to start with the big dream that makes

you want to jump out of bed singing every morning. Then, narrow it down to what you believe you can accomplish in a reasonable period of time — anywhere from a few months to a few years. Later, you can always reassess, but it's much better to aim too high than it is to settle for something you don't really care about or fail to give your biggest and best effort.

You only live once; why not make the most of it?

How Will You Know When You've Reached Your Goal?

The best goals have some degree of specificity to them. In fact, you should want yours to be as concrete as possible.

There are a couple of good reasons for this. The first is psychological. When you have a very firm idea of what dream you're trying to turn into a reality, you will be able to picture it clearly in your mind. You can form a concrete image of the way things look, feel, and maybe even taste or smell. That's going to count for a lot when you use visualization to reinforce the goal again and again.

The second reason is more practical. When your goals aren't specific enough, it's tough to know when you've reached them, or whether you're even on track to achieve them along the way. If there isn't a measurable outcome attached, then you're essentially moving in the right direction and hoping for the best. That's not terrible, if it gets you started, but gaining a sense of progress is very important when you're trying to remain motivated, and you can't do that if your goal is too vague.

How Long Will You Give Yourself to Achieve It?

Your goal should have some kind of time frame attached for the exact same reasons. You should be able to look at the calendar and say, "I expect to have reached my goal by this deadline." When that deadline is depends a great deal on what you're trying to do, and what sort of timing is realistic. What matters, though, is that you know when you can reasonably expect to have gotten there.

Again, there is a hidden motivating factor in here. Without any kind of deadline, the actions or habits needed to reach your goal could go on indefinitely. You aren't going to be motivated to change your behaviors, and stick with it through the inevitable setbacks, if there isn't any end in sight. If you can't be sure when or if you ever reach your goal, then how are you going to enjoy any sense of anticipation?

Also, remember that the gap between you and your dream lies in an actionable plan. A plan that stretches on forever doesn't have any specifics. It's just a wish list, or a set of activities leading toward an unknown conclusion. That's still better than taking no action at all, but it's certainly not a formula for motivation that's going to last for a long time.

Remember once again that you can always make your goals smaller for the time being, if that's what's needed to attach a deadline or make it realistic. It's much better to modify things, and keep working toward your ultimate goal, than it is to go after something you're not sure you can reach, or that may not be achievable on a schedule that's meaningful to you.

As a final note, the astute student of productivity books will recognize that I've essentially taken the very best from commonly used SMART goals and applied them to what we know about habits, motivation, and the subconscious mind. That's intentional. Big dreams are incredibly inspiring, but they have to be translated into workable visions before they can come to life. Once that happens, though, you're on the verge of accomplishing something special.

Nine

If You're Serious About Change, Take It One Step at a Time

Motivation is a bit like caffeine. A little bit of it gets you moving, but too much too quickly can actually be a bad thing.

As a case in point, consider what often happens following one of my motivational keynotes: At the conclusion, excited audience members who have never been shown the right way to change their attitudes and habits come up to me bright with ideas and enthusiasm. Then, they proceed to tell me about all the dozens of things they are going to start doing differently in the next few weeks.

I love the fact that they are so pumped up, and that they have a plan for achieving what used to seem out of reach. But I try to caution them not to take on too much at once. In fact, my advice is to prioritize their goals, choose the one that's most important at the moment, and begin with it first.

That can be tough advice to accept when you have many different issues you want to fix and improve in your life, or lots of personal and professionals goals you want to pursue. Still, it's a strategy I recommend because it works.

When you try to focus on too many different targets at the same time, your awareness of each of them is softened. You decrease the odds that you'll be able to accomplish anything, much less everything. Also, pursuing one goal requires a modest amount of willpower (at least if you're doing it in small, reasonable steps). As soon as you introduce more changes into the equation, the strain on your habits can get to be too much. You lose mental strength and find yourself being pulled back into existing routines. Change begins to feel painful and overwhelming once again.

In my view, it's much better to aim for one dominant goal at a time. If you can accept that to be a good guideline to follow, then it becomes a matter of narrowing it down to the one that makes sense to devote your time, energy, and focus to.

What Really Matters to You Right Now?

If you're like most of us, you probably have several overlapping or competing goals that you would like to meet in your personal and professional life. Perhaps you want to start your own business and work at it part time, get in shape to finish a 5K, and learn a new language so you can take a long trip overseas. These are just examples, of course, but they're representative of the kinds of personal wishes people share with me all the time.

You can pursue them all, but it's best not to try to do it all at once. So, you have to ask yourself: What matters right now? Which of these is a more intense or pressing need than the others? What will make me feel wonderful if I can achieve it?

Sometimes, just looking into your own emotions is enough to help you prioritize. One goal might stand out as being especially significant in your mind. Or it might just be easier to pay attention to in the short term. As difficult as it might feel to make that kind of assessment, see if you can choose one and bring some clarity to the situation. It doesn't mean you'll never reach the other goals, just that they won't be your first priority at the moment.

Start at the Natural Point

Could reaching one of your goals help you achieve the others? If so, it might be the perfect starting point.

To follow along with the example I gave above, starting your own part-time business might help you save up the money you need to travel overseas. Or, getting in shape by running might give you an extra boost of energy and confidence to help you grab hold of your entrepreneurial instincts. Maybe learning a language and taking a trip should come first, because you aren't sure whether you'll be able to take the time away from your growing business endeavor later.

In these kinds of situations, you may be able to find a natural starting point among your competing goals. That, in turn, can help nudge you in the right direction so you feel good about taking on one project and putting off the others for a little while. Nothing can get started until you begin working on one of your dreams, so if it will help feed into the others, that's even better.

Give Yourself a Win

A different way to evaluate your competing goals and set a priority is to simply think about which of your dreams would be easiest to reach in the short term. Assuming that it doesn't cause you to pass up on something that's more important, or personally meaningful, there's nothing wrong with giving yourself a win.

This is particularly true if you have struggled to motivate yourself or stick with your plans in the past. A lot of people have had their self-esteem crushed through years of trying different ideas without success. They get to the point where it's tough to take on a new challenge, much less feel any excitement about it. In those instances, earning a victory — and achieving one of your goals, even if it's a small one — can feel like a big deal.

Additionally, it's worth pointing out that success can become addictive (in a good way). Once you realize that you have hidden strengths, and really can improve your life when you try, you start to look ahead to the next victory. The first 5K leads to the first marathon. Someone who publishes a short story goes on to write a novel. A traveler leaving the country for the first time goes on to visit every continent.

Regardless of where you decide to begin, know that you have it in you to do great things. And, the better you get at finding achievable goals, concentrating on them, and seeing the results, the more likely you are to keep at it… and the bigger changes you'll see in your life as a result.

Ten

How to Reinforce Your Goals and Refuel Your Motivation

One reason motivated people seem to be so different from their friends and colleagues has to do with the fact that energy and momentum building increase over time. If you use a little bit of motivation today, you get more of it tomorrow, and so on. The trick, however, is that you have to keep yourself energized and focused for this process to take on a life of its own.

There are a lot of ways to get motivated for short bursts. You can pick up a book, watch a video, or attend a seminar and come away feeling like you're ready to take on the world. That feeling only lasts for a day or two at most, though, and then you're right back to where you were before. If you want to stay motivated, you have to reinforce a goal in your mind, keep triggering your emotions, and ensure your concentration doesn't waiver.

The best ways to do so all involve engaging your subconscious. That's the part of you that's going to feel things, move you to action, and override any intellectual doubts or fears you might have. Of course, changing your subconscious is harder than switching a conscious opinion, but it's far from impossible. You just have to know how to talk to yourself the right way.

Think in Pictures

You can reinforce your goal quickly and easily by stimulating your mind with the right visuals. Pictures are processed much more quickly and vividly by the brain than words are, and seeing reminders of what you want to accomplish can push you forward and energize you continuously.

This is particularly true if those images connect with you emotionally. If they make you feel excited, engaged, or ambitious, they'll touch you on a subconscious level and inspire you to think about your actions. That will make it easier to become aware of your existing habit, and to adopt new behaviors.

Using images to motivate yourself can be as simple as putting up pictures of the house you want to buy, looking at photos of yourself in a happy setting, or making a collage of images that reminds you of what you're trying to achieve. As long as you view them a few times a day — or better yet, put them somewhere you'll see them again and again — they'll make an impression on your inner mind.

Write It Down

There is a proven technique for reinforcing your goals that has been around for at least 100 years, and it's still as effective as ever: Three or four times a day, write out what it is you want to accomplish by hand a few times.

This is a simple strategy, but it's one that works. Writing down your goal forces you to access a different part of your brain, so you don't simply remember your goal; you interact with it mentally. That makes it more real and tangible to your subconscious, and greatly increases the odds you'll stay focused on it over time.

The key here, as with any strategy for imprinting conscious thoughts on the inner mind, lies in using emotion and repetition together. The more vividly you can picture yourself being successful (and feeling elated about it), the more powerful the image will become in your mind. Then, you just have to keep repeating the exercise until you are more focused than you've ever been in the past.

Engage in Quiet Reflection

Most adults don't realize just how powerful their imaginations are. They think they lose the ability to take themselves to other places in their minds once they stop being children, but the reality is they just start imagining differently.

This is easily demonstrated in a stage hypnosis show. Grown men and women can imagine just about anything, once they have become focused enough. The hard part is getting them to calm their conscious minds and pay attention to the right messages or suggestions.

With a little bit of quiet reflection — also known as mindfulness, meditation, or self-hypnosis — anyone can achieve the same kinds of results as I get in a show or presentation. All it takes is a willingness to concentrate on one thought at a time, and the practice of doing so again and again over the course of a few weeks.

If you want to give it a try, begin by sitting comfortably in a quiet space. See if you can tune out any distracting noises or sights, but don't worry too much about things you can hear in the background. When you feel ready, take a few deep breaths and close your eyes. Then, spend a minute or two thinking about your goal, about the steps involved in achieving it, and the feeling you'll have once you've made the breakthrough.

That exercise will most likely give you a warm, calm sensation. Follow it up by repeating, out loud or in your mind, that you're in the process of reaching your goal. Work at this until you can hear the conviction in your own voice, and feel the pride and happiness that come with achieving something that means so much to you.

It's likely that you'll find this exercise to be difficult at first. Most people have a hard time concentrating in silence for very long, especially in a world where attention spans are shrinking every day. Over time, though, you'll learn that you can tune out distracting thoughts or ideas, that your goals will become ingrained as a part of your everyday life, and that your powers of concentration will improve.

The motivation to reach your goals has to come from within, and it needs to be reinforced on a conscious and subconscious level repeatedly if you're going to become a master of motivation. Quick bits of inspiration come and go, but if you want to turn yourself into a driven achiever, you need a plan to fuel your mental engine again and again. Use these strategies to do that every day.

Eleven

Small Steps Can Lead to Big Changes in Your Life

One of the biggest challenges involved in setting and reaching a goal is finding the right balance between the desire to accomplish something big and the need to set realistic targets. Aim too low and you won't be inspired by your goal; set the bar too high and you'll lose your motivation when you realize you can't possibly be successful.

I feel the best way to get past this obstacle is to always be dreaming about accomplishing something big, while at the same time setting your sights on a goal or habit that's within reach from where you are currently. It's best to break things down into small steps, recognize what that first step might be, and then move forward.

That might be difficult if you're the kind of person who likes to move full speed ahead, but it's a system that's far more likely to lead you toward actually reaching your goal. There are several reasons to break down your goal into an immediate step.

Small Habits Are Easier to Keep

People are good at making decisions that will lead to major life changes… they just aren't great at sticking to them. How many men and women do you know who have decided to quit smoking cold turkey, get to the office an hour earlier, or lose 50 pounds? And how long are they usually successful?

In each case, it would have been easier to aim for incremental improvement. They could have cut back by one or two cigarettes a day, decided to leave for work 10 minutes earlier, or set their sights on losing five pounds as a starting point. The initial rush of emotion might not have been quite as huge, but they would have stood a much greater chance of sticking with the new habit.

When you turn your life upside down in an instant to do something new, you run a big risk of being overwhelmed and falling into old habits. But when you change one or two little things at a time, you give yourself a chance to ease into a new routine without feeling like you're trying to do everything at once.

Failure Is Discouraging

Looking at things from the other side of the coin, most of us will easily recognize that reaching a goal motivates you to set another one, while coming up short can make a person feel as if they don't want to try again the next time.

When you set a very big, all-or-nothing goal, you're practically inviting failure. By saying that you'll double your income in a year, or drop four sizes in a month, you leave open the possibility that you'll work hard and still not meet your goal because it just wasn't possible. Or, you could push so hard to reach the goal that you do something that will ultimately be harmful to your career or health.

Either way, having an unrealistic goal isn't going to be very motivating. The point of trying to improve isn't to make yourself perfect in a short period of time. Instead, it's to learn how you can manage change and get closer to the life you dream of living.

Little Changes Add Up

I used to remember my grandmother saying that a watched pot never wants to boil. The harder you stare at something while waiting for a certain result, the easier it is to miss progress toward that result.

That's because most progress is the result of small changes and incremental improvements. For an example of this, let's stay with the topic of weight loss. People following fad diets usually lose a few pounds, see their willpower disappear, and then gain it back (and sometimes more). But the person who substitutes water for soda at lunch and starts walking 20 minutes a day gets into better shape permanently.

This isn't because your body can't adjust quickly, but because big changes are mentally difficult. By setting new habits, you allow the process of change to gain momentum and accelerate. That's when improvements that once seemed impossible start to happen all by themselves.

One Thing Leads to the Next

Deciding to make a small change in your life doesn't mean you have to settle for only making a small change in your life. In fact, it's a way of telling yourself that you're in the journey for the long haul. It means you're serious about pursuing whatever is important to you, instead of just making yourself feel good for a few hours.

It's almost always the case that making a huge change turns out being a lot tougher than people think it will be, and that the results from small changes add up faster than they expect. When you can see that you're having one small success after another, it's easy to decide to do a little more and move on to the next step. But when you're stretching yourself every day to meet an impossible goal, it quickly becomes exhausting.

You can use today's small goal to generate a bit of momentum and motivate yourself to get started in the right direction. Then, you can reassess things after 30 or 60 days to figure out what the next reasonable step might be. Each transition will be easier that way, and you'll always be moving steadily toward your most important goal.

What's Your First Move Forward?

Knowing how beneficial it can be to break your biggest life goals down into small steps, how can you begin to reshape your life? What is the first move that makes sense?

If you already know, and the habit you have to adopt is a realistic one, then begin right away. Don't wait until the perfect moment because it won't ever come. Now is always a better time than later, because it's easy to put things off until you forget about them altogether. How many dreams and goals have died simply because the men and women who held on to them never simply decided to get started?

When you aren't sure how to begin, make finding that answer job number one. Learn what it would take to get closer to your target, and keep learning until you're sure you have a small habit to adopt. Once you know what you can do to start making realistic progress, you're on the path to success.

Tweleve

You Can Achieve Something Huge, One Day at a Time

If you're serious about achieving something that matters to you, don't just settle for breaking it down into small steps. Set a daily goal for yourself that will lead you toward the bigger progress you want to create without letting yourself get overwhelmed along the way.

What could you do each and every day that would bring you closer to reaching your dreams? How could you keep inching forward in a predictable way? When you can answer that question, you have the formula for lasting success. That's because you can achieve truly great and amazing things, so long as you're willing to take small steps one day at a time.

Find an Action That's Measurable, Repeatable, and Under Your Control

The distinction between small steps and daily targets is an important one. There are likely to be many, many different incremental actions that will be required if you're going to meet your dream. To get to the first one of those, however, you want to fall into a daily routine.

For the sake of illustration, let's suppose for a moment that your dream is to lose 50 pounds and run in the Boston Marathon. That might seem like an overwhelming goal from where you are right now. But you could say that the first small step would be participating in a local community 1-mile race or "fun run" that will be held in a few months. Knowing that, you could make it your daily goal to get up half an hour earlier each morning, stretch out, walk and jog for 10 minutes around your block, and then have a healthy breakfast.

You can take the same sort of template and apply it to any dream that you've broken into smaller steps. By turning something that seemed huge into a series of manageable accomplishments and daily actions, you could earn a new business certification, double your income, pick up a foreign language, or plan an amazing trip around the world. All that's required is a willingness to turn the process into milestones that makes sense, and then be willing to take action toward reaching them.

In the same way that your bigger goals should be SMART — and in particular, measurable and actionable — so should your daily targets. You'll note that in the example I gave above, jogging for 10 minutes is a realistic amount of effort that you could expect to put in just about every day. And, it's absolutely measurable and under your control. Suppose your daily target was to "always be on time." You might have a more difficult time staying on target with a goal like that because some delays are going to be outside your influence. Everyone is late once in a while. You can leave the house 15 minutes earlier, but you can't guarantee you'll arrive at your destination on time.

Likewise, if you decided your daily target was going to be 30 minutes of running, instead of 10 minutes of jogging, you might discover that the increased effort is just too much on a daily basis. You could wake up feeling sore or discouraged from the amount of work it was taking to reach your goal. In that case, you'd be setting yourself up for failure, because your daily action isn't repeatable. It's too much, too soon.

And finally, remember that your daily goal has to be something you can measure and record. I have had people tell me that the habit they want to set is one where they "wake up and feel great." Not only is this not completely within their control, but how would you go about measuring something like that? You can certainly adopt the mindset that you're going to be happy and healthy, but it's difficult for most people to definitively say they are going to feel a certain way regardless of what's going on with their bodies, what's happening in their careers, or what's going on in the world around them.

There's nothing wrong with adjusting your goals and mindset as you go. So, if you find your daily targets just aren't working for you, revisit these points to see if you can figure out what might be missing. Often, when people have a change they want to make in their lives, but are struggling to move forward, it's because they haven't taken the time to focus on a daily habit, or are thinking in the wrong terms. You want to be moving closer to the life you want every single day, and to do so by focusing on an action that's measurable, repeatable, and under your control.

Reinforce Your Habit 7 Days a Week If You Can

When you have a daily target, it's easy for you to stay on track and moving in the right direction. Better yet, you'll have a plan that will help you develop new habits that can quickly become a part of your daily routine. Any activity, performed with enough repetition over time, will become a habit and expectation.

Your subconscious mind can't distinguish between Monday and Saturday. You might get out of bed grudgingly at the start of a week, and influence your own emotions in that way, but when it comes to setting habits there isn't a qualitative difference between one day and the next. So, you should try to reinforce your daily habit throughout the week if you can. Even if you have to scale back on some days, or make a few adjustments in other areas of your life, see if you can take some time — or better yet, the same time each day — to move toward your goal.

This won't necessarily be easy at first, but that's why you want to be sure your daily goal is a realistic one, and not such a big task that you get overwhelmed or stressed out. The more regularly you can perform it, the easier it's going to be to form those crucial habits that are going to drag you forward toward your goal week after week.

Thirteen

Make Change Easier With Planning and Preparation

Anything you'll ever want to do in your life will get easier when you have the right plan in place to accomplish it. Simply thinking ahead to the decisions, tasks, and changes you'll have to face to reach your goal can help you spot opportunities and stumbling blocks.

Unfortunately, a lot of people decide to change, but never get around to planning how the change is actually going to happen. And so, instead of a realistic goal they can achieve, they end up with a wish that won't ever actually be fulfilled.

It's hard to build anything bigger than a sandwich without some kind of plan, and that's as true in our own minds as it is in the physical world. You don't need a complicated plan to set your life on a new course, but you should think ahead to figure out what kind of effort it will take to get you to the next level.

Plans Should Be Written and Recorded

It's well and good to know what your goal is and have an idea of how you want to go about accomplishing it in terms of daily effort, but that plan shouldn't be kept only in your mind. It will be much more powerful, compelling, and concrete if you have it written or saved somewhere.

One reason to keep your plan written is so you can keep track of it. Since you want a goal that's specific, realistic, measurable, and time-sensitive, it might take you a while to work backward and decide what it should be. Don't risk losing sight of the goal because you can't remember what it was supposed to say.

As important as remembering your goal is, though, it's even more important to be reminded about it on a daily basis. You want to see your new daily habit, and maybe even re-write it a few times, at regular intervals. That way it will be reinforced again and again so it can be absorbed into your subconscious mind. That can't happen if your goal only exists in your mind.

Don't Sabotage Your Own Efforts

It's hard enough to resist old habits and make changes in your life when things are planned and arranged in a way that makes sense. It's almost impossible if you start putting up roadblocks in your own path. Sadly, that's exactly what many people do.

Make things as easy as they can be. Don't decide you're going to lose 10 pounds and then schedule a cruise that's built around gourmet experiences. Clear your desk of video games, social notifications, and other distractions if you really need to study. Avoid the temptation to schedule a night on the town with your rowdiest friends if you need to be preparing for a business presentation.

Success doesn't happen by accident, and change rarely takes place on its own. If you want to be different tomorrow than you are today, plan ahead and don't let yourself become a victim of self-inflicted distractions and setbacks. Reaching your goals isn't nearly as hard as you think, but it's almost impossible if you make a habit of getting in your own way.

Decide What You'll Sacrifice

Usually, if you want to get something in life, you have to give up something else first. That's because each of us only has so much time, energy, and attention to go around. If we waste these resources on activities that aren't bringing us closer to what we really want, then we can't be surprised when we end up feeling stuck.

You can make the process of change much easier and more straightforward by simply deciding upfront what you're willing to give up to get what you want. The sacrifice that's required will depend a great deal on what you hope to achieve. Someone looking to get into shape will likely have to cut back on a few of their favorite treats. A person who desires to become an expert in his or her field might have to trade evenings on the couch watching TV for late nights hitting the books. To increase your productivity and income, it might be necessary to spend less time having coffee with your coworkers and more time talking to customers or managers.

Keep in mind that making sacrifices doesn't have to be an all-or-nothing proposition. You can decide you're going to get in shape, earn a promotion, go back to school, or meet any other personal or professional goal that's important to you and enjoy yourself. In fact, you may find that you enjoy your free time and leisure activities even more, since they have more value to you and you are becoming happier as you move closer to your goal. Just decide ahead of time what you're willing to give up, and by how much, so you can turn your dream into a reality.

Think Ahead to Your New Routine

Inevitably, what makes change hard isn't the act of doing something new, but altering your daily routine in a way that feels uncomfortable. You can prepare for this and increase your odds of successfully altering your daily habits at the same time by using a bit of visualization.

Simply imagine yourself facing a new day. Then, look ahead mentally to the moments where you'll have to do something different than you've done in the past. If your goal were to lose weight and become more athletic, that might mean ordering a different meal, choosing a healthier snack, or waking up early to exercise. Whatever you need to start doing, imagine that you have already made the change successfully. See what your new routine is like. How does it feel? What do you see or smell? What might others have to say about your new habits?

When you can hold this picture in your mind, go a step further. Think about the different temptations that might arise. Imagine you're being faced with a tough decision, feeling stressed, or being drawn back to your old habits. Now picture yourself moving toward the goal you want to reach anyway.

The changes you want to make in your life have to be made in your mind first. The more you can plan, prepare, and mentally acclimate yourself to a new reality, the easier it is to adjust and overcome the tendency to slide back to where you started.

Fourteen

You Don't Have to Conquer Every Challenge Alone

Goal setting and personal improvement are often thought of as individual events in the games of our lives, but why? You undoubtedly have friends, colleagues, and loved ones who would like to see you succeed and reach your goals, so why not turn to them for help?

In my experience, it often seems that people don't want to ask for help making changes in their lives because doing so would make them vulnerable. They'd have to admit that they aren't living up to their own dreams and expectations, that they have weaknesses, or that they have been holding on to bad habits for too long. These things are essentially true for everyone on the planet, but none of us likes to admit to it.

If you can get past this emotional stumbling block, there are some very big benefits to getting others involved in your process of change. In an instant you'll find you have more encouragement and support than you might have imagined.

You really don't have to conquer every challenge alone, and things are easier and more rewarding when you don't.

Bringing Bad Habits Into the Light

We all want our colleagues and loved ones to think about us in a positive way. So talking to them about our bad habits can be difficult. But, when we bring them into the light, we gain a powerful tool for overcoming them.

By sharing our goal with other people — and letting them know what we're trying to give up as part of that goal — we almost always get the admiration of others. They love that we are willing to push ourselves forward to get better than we currently are, and are likely to offer their help. They might give us pointers, words of encouragement, tales of their own trials, or even incentives.

Any of these would be reason enough to share your goals with others. But there are a couple of other benefits that are just as powerful. The first has to do with the fact that saying something out loud to other people makes it more real to you, and to your subconscious mind. It creates a kind of commitment. You aren't just thinking about doing something; you're actually making a go of it.

Occasionally, the inverse will be true and you'll have a friend or family member who won't support you. In fact, they'll tell you all the reasons they think it's impossible to make the kind of change or improvement you're planning. That's fine. Don't be discouraged, because they've shared with you the reasons why they can't be successful, not definitive proof that you won't be.

Emotionally Engaging Your Inner Mind

Psychologically speaking, fear can be more powerful than ambition. We tend to be hurt more by losing what we have than we are by failing to get what we want. Given that our subconscious minds respond so readily to emotion, we can use this dynamic to trick ourselves into being more motivated than we ever have been in the past.

By sharing your plans with someone else whose respect you want to earn or keep, you make yourself accountable. Often, that in and of itself will be enough to keep you moving forward, since you won't want the other person to think of you as a quitter. You'll know that they are likely to ask you about your goal, and the progress you're making. So, you may keep pushing ahead just so you won't have to admit defeat or backtrack on the commitment you made.

The closer another person is to us, the more we tend to be motivated by a sense of accountability to them. In the same way that you wouldn't want to tell your boss you'd finish an important project by the end of the week and then fail to deliver, you probably aren't going to give up on a goal that you've mentioned to your spouse, your best friend, or your kids very quickly. That's one way you can use your emotions to become a better, more productive version of yourself.

Keeping the Wrong Influences Away

When it comes to the process of goal setting and involving others, a word of caution needs to be issued. That's because not everyone in your life is probably going to be proud, impressed, and encouraging when they find out you want to do something meaningful.

More often than not, it doesn't have anything to do with you. Instead, it's all about the fact that they are afraid to make changes in their own lives, or have tried and failed in the past. When they see you striving for something bigger and better, they might have to confront a weakness or shortcoming in themselves, or may worry that you're not going to have time for them anymore. They might even wonder if a successful change will mean you won't want to see them.

When these situations arise, there are a couple of steps you can take. The first is to explain how important the new habit or dream is to you, and to ask them for their support. You might even go farther and invite them to make a change with you so that the two of you can improve together and enjoy the benefits. Or, if that isn't possible, you can minimize your contact with them while you're trying hard to set your new habit. It might not be easy, but you shouldn't let someone else's negativity infect you to the point that you're afraid to pursue your own dreams. Believe me, that's an easier and more common trap than you might realize.

Just about any person you spend time with is going to have a positive or negative effect on your life, your dreams, and your emotions. Your true friends and loved ones are going to want to lift you up and see you be successful. They're going to offer encouragement, compliments, and support when you need it most. As for the others, remember what your mother always told you: If they don't want to see you happy, then they probably weren't real friends in the first place.

Fifteen

To Get Moving, You Have to Get Started First

There is an interesting tug-of-war that sometimes takes place in people's minds when they think about motivation, goal setting, and personal change. On the one hand, planning ahead and making preparations is key to being successful. It's hard to overcome bad habits and existing patterns if you don't have a good strategy in place. But on the other hand, it's easy to spend too much time thinking and planning when you should be doing.

Believe it or not, there comes a point where reaching your most important goals is easy. You simply make a small habit and keep working at it until it becomes ingrained. Then, it's so natural to do the new thing that you can't imagine going back to your old routines. Suddenly, you're moving steadily toward the outcome you want, and feeling like you're putting in less effort than ever. You are literally being guided in the right direction toward the life you want.

The caveat is that none of that can happen until you get started. All the plans, strategies, and knowledge in the world won't help you if you don't take the first step and turn your inspiration into action. That's an area where many of us come up short, so we should look at a few insights that make it easier to nudge ourselves in the right direction.

Nothing Gets Easier With Procrastination

A funny thing happens when you put a job off for a while. What initially seemed simple suddenly turns into a complex and overwhelming task. There are a number of psychological reasons for this, but the biggest one has to do with decision fatigue. The longer you let a task or item sit at the back of your brain, the more unpleasant it becomes. So a job that would have been simple when you started can feel like a major chore.

Nothing gets easier when you procrastinate. There are always reasons not to do something right now, and dwelling on these reasons will make your goal seem far away and impossible. In contrast, when you take the first step toward changing your life for the better, you break through an invisible barrier. You do something differently, even if it's something small and momentary, and notice that the world didn't fall apart. Rather than having a mindset of defeat be reinforced upon your subconscious, you are suddenly reminded that it really is up to you to set the course for your future.

It's not unusual for the decision to make a change in your life to be harder than the change itself. Putting things off makes them seem difficult, while working on them sets your mind off in a new direction and gives you more motivational fuel. To make your new habits as easy as possible, set your goals, figure out how to start reaching them, and then take action right away before that feeling fades.

Start With Where You Are Now

It's not unusual for people to make the process of change conditional. They'd love to get busy doing something new, they'll tell you, but they don't have the time or money needed to put their ideas into action.

The reality is that these kinds of qualifiers are almost always excuses. Whatever your biggest and most important goal in life is, there are things you can do right now to either turn it into a reality or get moving in the right direction. You don't need a million dollars, a pair of new shoes, or five more hours in the day. Instead, you just need a different attitude.

Given that little changes are usually more substantial than big ones anyway, it only makes sense to begin with whatever you can work with right now. You can always devote more time, money, or attention to the job later. For now, getting started is more important than getting everything perfect.

There Is Always a First Step

Depending on what your dream or goal looks like, the first step might not be an obvious one. You may be a bit confused as to the best way to move forward, and wary of taking any action that could be expensive, time-consuming, or counterproductive later on. So how can you get started if you don't know where the starting line is?

Begin by recognizing that the obstacle might not be as substantial as you think it is. Often, when someone says they don't have to get started toward reaching their dream, it's because they (consciously or subconsciously) are procrastinating. They are afraid of failure, or success, and the "I don't know what to do" excuse is a convenient one. Ask yourself whether you're really confused, or if you're just afraid to face what you want out of your life. If you come to the conclusion that it's really hesitation that's holding you back, move up a few paragraphs, read the bit about procrastination again, and then get started.

If you truly are stumped, that's fine. You're still in luck, because there has never been so much information and advice available to you in the history of mankind. You can go online, pick up the phone, or even visit a local library and find the answers you need. There may be experts who are down the block, or just a click away, and they'll be glad to help you get started. They may even have (or be able to point you to) learning tools like blog posts, YouTube clips, and other free resources. If you don't know what the first step toward reaching your dream is, then finding that out becomes your first step. Do it now, and then get started in earnest.

And finally, remember that no one ever takes a straight line to success. At a certain point, you just have to make the best decision you can, even if it means you'll wish you had done some things a little bit differently in the future. Getting started now is always preferable, even if it means making a few mistakes. If you wait for things to be just right, or to have the perfect piece of information in hand, you'll never get going.

Sixteen

To Reach Your Goals, Set a System of Rewards and Punishments

If you want to make any big and important change in your life, you can follow a simple process. First, you determine what goal really matters to you most in the moment. Then, you reduce that goal down to a simple daily habit that you expect will lead you to success. And finally, you follow through with that habit again and again until you find yourself living the kind of life you were hoping for and move on to the next goal.

More often than not, it's the middle part of that equation that gives people trouble. They know how to set goals, and love thinking about the way their lives will be once they reach them. When it comes to following through with their new daily habits and routines, however, they tend to struggle. They run out of willpower and quickly find themselves back where they started, only feeling a little more discouraged than they were in the past.

Luckily, I'm going to pass on a handy trick you can use to reinforce those daily habits and motivate yourself in a powerful way. To do so, I'm going to turn to an old friend of mine: basic classical psychology.

Reaching Your Inner Mind the Easy Way

If you have ever taken a psychology class, then you might remember that humans — like all living organisms — tend to move toward pleasure and away from pain. That makes perfect sense, but it's also the biggest reason people have trouble changing. Adopting a new habit or routine feels painful, so our minds drag us back to old routines that feel comfortable.

There is a way to flip this dynamic around, though. When trying to set a new habit, reward yourself instantly for completing a task or action that moves you closer to your goal. For instance, if you wanted to finish a novel, you could buy yourself an expensive cup of coffee every time you wrote a new page. If your goal were to lose 10 pounds, you could reward yourself with an extra piece of chocolate after running a few miles. An aspiring executive could put away a few dollars toward a dream vacation each time they made a new networking contact.

These are simple examples, but they illustrate an important idea: By giving yourself a reward for successfully completing a daily goal, you associate the action or event with pleasure instead of pain. The "good" of your treat outweighs the “bad” of the changed routine.

Naturally, as you might imagine, the alternative works just as well. That is, if you have a daily habit you’re trying to reinforce and you don’t meet your own expectations, you give yourself a punishment. Failing to write the pages could mean you can’t buy a new book. Skipping your run could equal salad for dinner. Missing out on your networking goal takes away the contribution you were going to make to your vacation fund and compels you to delete a favorite TV show without watching it.

This type of system is simple, but it can work incredibly well. Our brains are trained to seek rewards and avoid punishments. Why not use what you know about your own psychology to motivate yourself on a daily basis?

The 3 Ingredients for a Reward and Punishment System

Your scheme for rewards and punishments doesn’t have to be complicated. To increase your odds of success, though, there are a few guidelines you should follow.

The first is that your rewards and your punishments both need to be simple. A cookie might make a good reward, or half an hour spent on an enjoyable activity. The more elaborate, expensive, or time-consuming your reward or punishment is, the harder it’s going to be to follow through. Make things easy by picking something straightforward that you know you can stick to.

The second detail is that your rewards and punishments need to be meaningful to you personally. Goals that don't excite you emotionally aren't motivating; your subconscious mind simply won't pay attention unless you feel strongly about something. The same principle applies when it comes to rewards and punishments. You have to really want your goal if it's going to motivate you to complete your daily task, and really fear or dislike your punishment if it's going to keep you in line. Again, adhere to terms of complexity or severity, but pick something that matters to you and you'll achieve much better results.

And finally, for this motivational tactic to have any effect, you have to actually follow through with your rewards and punishments. You can't simply decide you deserve your reward even though you didn't meet your goal, or skip your punishment because you don't feel like doing it. Involve others for accountability if you need to, but follow through either way, because that's what's going to make an impression on your inner mind.

A Pavlovian Formula for Goal Achievement

Even men and women who have never taken a psychology class have heard of Pavlov's dogs, and tend to know that they represent an easy way to grasp the power of classical conditioning. Your brain might be bigger than a canine's, but the part of it that motivates you most strongly works in almost exactly the same way.

Although using rewards and punishments might seem like a simple or gimmicky way to help you adopt a new habit, trust me when I tell you it works. You might not even be conscious of the difference it's making, but on some level, your mind will push you toward the pleasurable rewards (and away from the self-imposed punishments) with more and more intensity the longer you stay at it. Even if you start to get used to your punishment, a certain part of your brain will dread it, and push you to achieve your goals so you can have a reward instead.

It takes the average person somewhere between three and five weeks to set a new permanent habit. By using a system of rewards and punishments, you'll be able to accelerate this process and make it more meaningful to your subconscious mind. Once that happens, you'll be an unstoppable motivation machine!

Seventeen

If You Want to Stay Motivated, Keep Score

As I'm fond of pointing out, setting and reaching your goals involves a bit of a Catch-22 dilemma. On the one hand, big goals are the most motivating, because they inspire us and engage us on emotional level that resonates with our subconscious minds. But on the other hand, the only way to reach your biggest goals with any level of certainty and consistency is to break them into very small steps and daily habits. So, most people feel a rush of motivation and willpower when they set a goal, but find that it disappears when they actually get into the daily grind of reaching it.

One way to break out of that cycle, keep motivated, and prevent setbacks is to keep score. That is, you should be tracking your daily, weekly, and monthly progress so you can see where you've been and where you're going all at the same time.

There are any number of ways to keep score when it comes to personal achievement. You can turn to spreadsheets, handwritten notes, or any one of a dozen different mobile apps that will help you track your activity. How you keep tabs on your progress isn't nearly as important as the fact that you do so. I want to share with you a few of the reasons why this is such an important concept, and how it can make or break your plans for personal change.

Small Decisions Get Easier When You Track Them

As anyone who's ever gotten serious about losing weight could tell you, a cornerstone of nearly every fitness plan is keeping a journal that shows what you ate, how much exercise you performed, and so on. This is partly beneficial because it helps you understand your personal patterns and see the ways they can shape and influence your weight over time. Just as important, however, is that the active record-keeping changes your behavior itself.

In other words, when you know you're going to have to enter your daily meals into an app and add up your calories, you suddenly become less likely to indulge in things like chocolate cake and sugary coffee drinks. You don't want to include those in your tally, which persuades you to skip them in the first place.

Lots of small decisions get easier, and lots of everyday temptations seem a lot less powerful, when you are keeping track of the progress you're making toward your goal. The example I gave for fitness is a good one that most people can relate to, but the same principle works when you're recording sales calls, client meetings, the number of cigarettes smoked, or anything else relating to an important personal habit. Something that you might have done unconsciously in the past seems a lot less compelling when you know you'll have to own up to it later.

Good Notes Help You Spot Patterns

Another benefit of keeping track of your daily actions is that it can help you spot trends, patterns, and obstacles over time. For instance, you may note that you often feel tired on Saturday and miss a workout, or that Monday afternoons are when you tend to get more overwhelmed than usual at work.

Having this kind of insight is crucial. And sadly, it's something most of us go without. In my experience, the vast majority of men and women who struggle to make changes in their own lives often feel as if they are drifting from one event or circumstance to the next. They have plans, but those plans never come to fruition because they feel like they are constantly being blown off course. When they can take a step back, however, and look at the kinds of routines that are keeping them locked in place, it suddenly becomes much simpler to overcome them.

By just keeping good notes, you may discover that you need to go to bed earlier on Friday, set aside some time on

Monday morning to work on your most important project, or take some other action that can help you preempt a setback before it ever takes place. The better your records are, the easier it's going to be for you to find ways to move ahead and stay on track to reach your goals.

Nothing Motivates Like Progress

Finally, it's a good idea to keep track of the progress you're making simply because the small steps you are taking are going to add up more quickly than you realize. In fact, we tend to be our own worst critics simply because we don't have an outside perspective on the efforts we are making.

To stick with an easy and visible example of this phenomenon at work, consider what happens when you lose two or three pounds. Many of us wouldn't notice a visible change by looking into a mirror. By counting calories and weighing ourselves daily, though, we can spot incremental signs of progress before they become visible to the naked eye. That, in turn, makes us want to keep going… rather than feeling like the hard work we are putting in isn't paying off and convincing ourselves to give up too soon.

Nothing has the power to motivate you like being able to see that you're actually moving toward the life you want to be living. When you can look at your notes and see where you began, how far you've come, and that there is a breakthrough within sight, you'll be a lot more likely to keep going when things get tough. And, no matter how well you've defined your goals, and how meaningful they are to you, you probably will run into occasions where building momentum feels difficult.

When you keep track of what you're doing, everything about the goal setting and achievement process gets easier. It only takes a minute or two each day to record your activity, so make a habit of noting what you've done to change your life, no matter how small or incremental it might seem. And once you do, be sure to give yourself a pat on the back, because you have done something most people won't by taking action to get what you want most.

Eighteen

How to Handle Bumps on the Road to Success

I would love to tell you that, once you have the right goal setting and mental motivation plan, everything in your life is going to resolve itself immediately. And, if that's what you really want to read, there are dozens and dozens of books out there with that essential message. But, you and I would both know better. No matter how much planning, willpower, and emotion you put into reaching your goal, there are likely to be setbacks. And for that reason, one of the most important elements of change isn't avoiding trouble, but learning how to handle bumps on the road to success.

You've heard it a thousand times: Anyone can start moving toward their goals and keep going when things are easy. Only the truly driven succeed when life and circumstances get in the way.

That's an entirely true sentiment, but one that's often misunderstood. Because willpower and motivation are different things, the way to deal with a setback isn't to just bear it and push forward. Instead, you have to have a plan for overcoming the inevitable so you won't be caught off guard when things aren't going your way. Let's take a look at a few of the things you have to know to keep moving when you aren't hitting your daily goals, or change starts to feel more difficult than it used to.

Change Is a River, Not a Highway

At the risk of beating this point to death, you have to know that your plan is just a plan. You're going to have to deviate from it at times, and life isn't going to cooperate simply because you want it to.

A lot of motivational experts and gurus preach that the law of attraction will bring you the things you most want and concentrate your energies on. There is a certain truth to this, in so far as your mind is a wonderful tool for planning and visualizing when you focus it tightly enough. But, expecting that you aren't going to run into any trouble simply because you want something intensely is going to leave you disappointed. Even worse, it can cause you to convince yourself that your goal isn't a good one simply because it's hard to reach.

Nothing could be further from the truth. The fact of the matter is that change is a river, not a highway — it has twists and turns, and it runs rough at times. Study the life of any ultra-successful person, and you'll find that they had to overcome adversity, usually several times. Instead of giving up, they refined their approach and got stronger. You can do the same, so long as you know that the tough times are going to come and you can't always prevent them. Be prepared for choppy waters, keep track of your progress, and know that you're going to drift off course on occasion.

Diagnose Problems as They Arise

As I've already noted, lots of men and women like to ignore setbacks and pretend that they either don't exist or won't happen. Even when they're in the midst of tough times, they want to keep persevering because they think it's the right thing to do.

This attitude is one that often lands people in emergency rooms and therapists' offices. They feel a twinge of pain when starting a new exercise program, for example, but don't want to give up, so they keep pushing ahead until they are truly too hurt to continue. Their grit is admirable, but where does it get them in the end?

A better approach is to diagnose your problems and failures as they arise. If you're coming up short when it's time to meet your daily goals, ask yourself whether the issue was a one-time distraction or something bigger. If you are keeping good notes and records of your daily activity, you should start to see trends emerge. Is there a part of your plan that's too challenging or just not possible at the moment? Is the goal you have set for yourself not motivating enough?

Or, have circumstances changed, meaning you need to revisit your approach?

At times, you'll be able to brush off a setback and keep moving ahead without reading much into it. However, by diagnosing your problems on a daily or weekly basis, you decrease the odds that you'll miss the forest for the trees and end up ruining your own motivational plan by focusing too tightly on any one detail.

Two Strategies to Get Back on Track

Generally speaking, there are two ways you can deal with a failure when it comes to reaching your daily goals or achieving a milestone on the way to success. You can either forget about it and move on, or increase your efforts to make up lost ground. There are positives and negatives to both approaches.

Depending on how big or important the goal was, and how often you find yourself coming up short, the best thing to do might be to simply chalk it up to a bad day or week, acknowledge that there were circumstances out of your control, and move on. You can simply begin again where you left off next time, letting the setback roll off of you while knowing you'll be a little wiser and more determined in the future. In most cases, this is going to be the best approach, particularly if you've set up a system of personal rewards and punishments that are helping you shape your behavior and habits over time.

Once in a while, though, it makes sense to stay on track by pushing yourself a little harder in the short term. If your goal were to start earning more money, for example, and you were late to work, you might decide to put in a few extra hours at the office during the evening or on a weekend. You don't want to push so hard that you use up all of your willpower and become discouraged, but it might be worth it if it helps you stay on track to achieve a bigger dream. Nothing is as motivating as making progress forward, so don't discount the value of a little extra effort here and there to come back from a shortcoming.

Either of these strategies can work, and it's up to you to figure out which one makes sense for your goal and situation. What you never want to do is turn a small setback into a stopping point.

The Difference Between a Setback and a Failure

Even the most driven individuals suffer setbacks when trying to reach their goals. They have injuries, illnesses, and family emergencies. They see their careers changed by outside events and the ups and downs of the economy. They question their own abilities, and suffer periods of low confidence and motivation just like the rest of us.

In fact, the biggest difference isn't in the number of hardships they endure, but in the way they think about them. That is, they know that the only difference between a setback and a failure is in how you respond. A setback temporarily halts your progress, while a failure occurs when you give up.

So long as you can keep that distinction clear in your mind, and stay focused on your long-term goal, nothing is going to stop you from reaching your dreams. There are always going to be obstacles along the way, but they never have to be final. Don't expect any important achievement to come too easily, and don't give up until you've gotten exactly what you want from the parts of your life that matter most to you.

Nineteen

No Goal Is Permanent: When to Reset or Reassess Your Plans

A lot of people tend to think of goal setting in concrete terms. In their minds, you make a goal, work toward it, and (hopefully) achieve it, after which the process is over.

There's nothing inherently wrong with this view, but it's a little bit limited when we think of the way actual achievement tends to work. Even setting aside the issue of setbacks and detours, it's important to recognize that goals can change, be reset, or end up being replaced along the way. And, all of this can happen without the original effort being a waste or a failure. After all, if trying to reach something doesn't work out, but still brings you closer to being happy and fulfilled, then wasn't it worth the effort?

I could refer to an almost endless number of reasons why you might decide to change your goals before you've actually achieved them. Let's take a look at a few of the most common and important ones.

Your Immediate Goal Should Never Be Too Easy or Too Hard

Setting the right goals is a balancing act between ambition and realism. You want to stretch yourself, so you can make progress toward the life you're trying to build, but without going so far that you feel like your target is out of reach and you can't motivate yourself to try.

If you find your immediate goal is too easy, then you aren't really doing all you could be to improve your life. Making any kind of start is better than making none at all, but you should feel like you're being challenged. Otherwise, you might not make the sort of progress you're hoping for over a longer time horizon, and that can start to eat away at your enthusiasm. Nobody likes to feel as if they are spinning their wheels, especially when they are working toward a dream.

Likewise, a daily goal that's too big and intimidating usually turns out to be daunting rather than energizing. The human mind is only equipped to handle so much change at once. Go beyond that, and it's easy to slip back into the comfort of old habits. When you set yourself up to think that some daily target is the one you have to reach to keep going forward, and then you find you can't do that thing day after day, it's easy to give up.

All things considered, it's probably better to have a daily target that's slightly too easy over one that's a bit too difficult, but there's nothing wrong with changing your plans either way to find the right fit. Sometimes, you don't know whether something will be simple or difficult until you've begun, so you might have to monitor your progress and make small course corrections as needed.

When Your Goal Stops Being Meaningful, It Stops Being a Motivator

Change feels hard because our minds don't want to accept new patterns when they don't have to. They will, if we choose the right goals and reinforce new habits again and again, but only if we feel personally and emotionally invested. When we try to take on a new idea, routine, or belief simply because we think we should, it doesn't move us to action.

This is an important detail about the subconscious you have to keep in mind, because a goal that's no longer meaningful isn't going to be a powerful motivator. If you lose your passion for a particular dream or idea, you aren't going to be able to push yourself to do the hard work to achieve it.

The solution to this issue is twofold. First, it requires that we continually refuel our own motivation by visualizing our goals, leaving ourselves reminders of what we want to achieve, and taking the time to review our progress. And second, it means it's necessary for us to check in with ourselves from time to time — especially following an important milestone or setback — and ask whether the goal we are chasing is really the one we want. If it isn't, then we

need to start moving in a new direction.

In the world of investments, you often see people "throw good money after bad" simply because they don't want to give up on an idea they once believed in. When it comes to personal development, the same principle applies, except it's time and energy that are being spent. If you have to let go of a goal that's no longer relevant, don't fight the impulse. Instead, move toward whatever it is that makes you want to jump up with excitement, because that's going to be the target that energizes you to achieve wonderful things.

First Things First

When it comes to making progress in your biggest goals, action beats contemplation almost every time. And yet, trying something new requires us to go outside our comfort zones. And when that happens, it's only natural for us to make missteps. In that way, you may find that what you thought was a logical starting point leads you to a different beginning, or even a dead end.

If that happens while you're on your way to reaching your goal, just take it in stride. Accept that there are some things you can't know when you're beginning, and that you'll have to figure them out as you go along. That's not the worst news in the world, because it means every step is making you just a little bit smarter and savvier than you were before.

No goal is ever permanent. Either you'll reach it, change it, or adjust your focus somewhere along the way. While that might seem like bad news to some, the reality is that the world belongs to those who take action and stay focused on their next move, not the people who become so entrenched in their routines that they can't make adjustments when they need to.

better adapted you're going to be for a world that is constantly in flux.

Twenty

Celebrating Your Victories Is Part of the Goal-Setting Process

For all of the reminders we get that change is hard, it's easy to forget that it isn't all about struggle and overcoming obstacles. In fact, one of the most important motivational tools you have is the ability to celebrate, cut loose, and take it easy once in a while. These diversions and days off are both helpful and necessary. Without them, you'd begin to feel like a robot instead of a motivated individual. That wouldn't just take the fun out of things; it would be counterproductive.

There's no point in reaching your goals if you can't savor your successes. It shouldn't be a surprise, then, that the two often go hand-in-hand. How and when do you celebrate your victories, and how does time spent away from your goals help motivate you to reach them? Let's look at the answers one by one.

Everybody Needs Downtime

Regular rest and maintenance are important for your body and your mind. Willpower comes in limited quantities, and it's extremely taxing to constantly find yourself obsessing over a current target or idea you are working toward. Motivation and focus are good; tunnel vision is bad.

The news is filled with examples of men and women who suddenly "snap," losing their cool because they have been holding their feelings and desires in for so long. Once they let go, they almost immediately begin to feel better. Usually, they just need a chance to release the pressure. As positive as the process of setting and reaching your goals can be, it's not going to do you much good to chase your dreams if you go overboard.

Knowing that, you should take care to work a bit of downtime into your calendar. Make sure you are rewarding yourself continually when you reach your daily goals, and don't be afraid to take a bit of time off or away when it's necessary. Athletes need rest days, dieters crave "cheat meals," and even workaholics usually find they can think more clearly after a long weekend spent on the beach. Everyone needs downtime at regular intervals, so give in to your natural impulse to feel good, reflect on your achievements, and take some time off once in a while.

Why Celebrations Are Motivating

When you reach a major goal or milestone, don't let the event pass you by without making it into an occasion. Buy yourself a gift, go out for a nice meal, or share your victory with others. These kinds of celebrations aren't just deserved; they can help keep you pushing forward.

One reason celebrations can be real motivators has to do with the emotional high you get from reaching your goal. We all love a sense of accomplishment. Our minds crave it. And once we get a taste, we want to duplicate that feeling again. So, when we pause to enjoy the reality of what we've done, we are also programming ourselves to go higher, farther, and faster.

Additionally, the reward we give ourselves for meeting an important goal can be motivating on its own. Tell yourself that you'll take a dream vacation if you get a big bonus at work, for example, and you'll be emotionally driven to meet that goal. You can still decide to put some of that money in savings, or pay your bills, but grab on to a reward that truly excites you. That will help reinforce all of the other motivational work you are doing.

You should also share your moment of glory with others, if you can. Not only will they potentially be inspired by what you've done and think about taking on a bigger goal for themselves, but the congratulations and admiration they send your way will further influence your subconscious mind. You'll love the fact that they are thinking good things about you, and that will help motivate you to reach the next target.

Putting all of these details together, it makes sense to plan your rewards and celebrations ahead of time. Give yourself something to look forward to, and leave room in your budget or calendar to enjoy it when you're done. That will ensure you don't get so busy planning your next goal that you forget to stop and enjoy the moment.

Don't Make Celebrations Counterproductive

A word of caution should be given when it comes to using celebrations and rewards as motivational tools: Namely, that you don't want them to become counterproductive.

The classic example of this is the person who celebrates losing 20 pounds by binge eating their favorite foods for a weekend. It might feel good for a little while, but ultimately it moves them backward in their quest to be healthier, and might leave them feeling bad about themselves. Had they celebrated by buying some new clothes instead, they might have been more motivated to stay in shape rather than moving backward. Similarly, some people will celebrate their freedom from debt by making a major purchase (such as a new car). That just leads them back to feeling as they did in the past, and forces them to start the process all over again.

Giving yourself a small treat or indulgence when you reach your goal is perfectly fine. In general, though, you want your celebration or reward to be something that supports your achievement and your new lifestyle, instead of taking you in the wrong direction. Everyone needs downtime, and a chance to celebrate the things they've worked so hard to achieve. The key is to do it the right way so you can stay motivated and build toward your next major goal.

Twenty One

When You Reach One Goal, It's Time to Set Another

What happens when you set up a huge goal for yourself, follow a mental motivation plan to change your daily habits, and then eventually reach it? I'll tell you what the most successful people I've ever met do: They celebrate their big win, take a little bit of time to reflect on how far they've come and what is most meaningful to them going forward, and then they set an even bigger goal and start working toward that.

Following that kind of process is the difference between achieving one big breakthrough in your life and using what you've learned to find happiness and fulfillment again and again. The people who are at the top of their careers, are in great physical shape, and manage to fulfill their personal dreams don't have any of these things happen by accident. Instead, they set goals, turn them into actionable plans, and then keep building toward bigger and more meaningful achievements. From the outside, it looks like all of this happens naturally, but that's rarely the case.

By the time you reach this stage in the goal-setting process, choosing another target and moving toward it will be the most natural thing in the world. You probably won't face many obstacles, because you'll feel like seeing how much farther you can go. However, there are a few things worth pointing out, even when it seems like you've made it to the top of the mountain.

Keep the Momentum Going

Big victories in life deserve big celebrations. It's possible to get so wrapped up in your victory lap, however, that you unintentionally set new habits that aren't taking you anywhere. As important as it is to get some downtime and acknowledge major milestones, you don't want the relaxation phase to go on for so long that it becomes your new normal.

In many cases, you might have an idea of what your next goal should look like already. Or, you might want to choose something that builds upon your previous success (if you ran a marathon, you might want to attempt a triathlon; if you started a business, maybe your aim is to see that business grow). Regardless of what it is you plan to do next, try to keep the momentum going and take action in a reasonable amount of time. That will keep you feeling engaged and energetic, and stop you from becoming so comfortable that you don't grow anymore.

As difficult as it is to get started and stay motivated when moving toward your goals, complacency can be a real concern after you've reached them. It's okay to be happy, and even satisfied. But, as long as you have more things to do and try in your life, you should never be completely content.

Look for Balance in Your Life

Another risk to reaching your goals has to do with the fact that each time you check off a major milestone, you become more and more invested in a certain part of your life. When you get promoted, your career takes center stage. If you master a musical instrument, you might want to join a band. Become an expert in something, and you'll want to keep learning about it.

These are all great instincts, but you have to keep an eye on them. That's because it's easy to pull your life out of focus unintentionally. By paying too much attention to one thing, you can neglect another — like your family, your health, or your other long-term goals — to the point of making yourself unhappy. A focused mind is a great thing, but a life that's built entirely around one particular pursuit or passion will often become lonely and empty.

A good rule of thumb is to make sure every fourth or fifth goal you set goes away from the others you've pursued recently. So, if the last year or two of your life has been structured for professional success, indulge your hobbies and personal relationships. Or, if you've been working hard at getting in shape, learn a new skill for a while as you tamp down your training and let your body heal. These are simple examples that won't apply to everyone, but the guiding idea is important. Look for balance in your life, and you'll be more fulfilled and productive with each new target you set for yourself.

Achievement Is an Addiction

Most people never realize this, but there is such a thing as a positive addiction. And I strongly believe that achievement is one of them.

Something magical and profound happens when you set a goal for yourself and then realize you can achieve it. The sense of accomplishment that arrives when you do something that once felt impossible can be put into words. It's simply overwhelming. When it subsides, you find yourself wanting to experience that emotion again as often as possible. And in that way, you can become addicted to success. At that point, a lot of the old relationships, bad habits, and distractions that used to seem so important just don't seem to matter anymore. You become focused on finding and achieving the next goal, and sharing what you've learned with others who have the same values.

This is an addiction I hope you acquire. It's one that can change your life, your mindset, and your entire perspective in a permanent way. Take the time to set your goals and then reinforce them. Change will come slowly at first, but you will reach your goals if you are determined enough and have the right plan. Once that happens, you might just find you have a taste for winning, and that your new appetite for success can take you to heights you hadn't ever dreamed of.

Conclusion

You Can Master Motivation Starting Today

I've shared a lot of simple ideas with you in this book, many of them overlapping or building on one another. That's intentional. Most people don't understand the way motivation and basic psychology work, so they think of self-improvement as something that's either impossible or an accidental event. The reality is much different: If you want to change your life, you just need to find a goal that excites you, a plan that will take you from where you are now to where you want to be, and the resolve to get started today.

If you have each of these, almost nothing can stop you. You might have setbacks, false starts, and changes in course, but you're going to do something that very few people ever do, which is go from a state of unhappiness to one of satisfaction.

It's unfortunate, but most people are comfortable complaining about their problems, while at the same time being completely unwilling to do anything about them. They like to think that their health, finances, and ambitions all exist in a realm that's outside their control, when a simple adjustment to their daily habits would take them toward the fitness, prosperity, and lifestyle they aspire to. They are afraid to face up to their own dreams and make a choice to change, and as a result the change never comes.

My hope is that you will be different. By making your way through these pages, you've given yourself a simple and straightforward set of tools you can use to achieve virtually anything you set your mind to. Whether you use them or not is entirely up to you. I can only tell you from years of experience and research that they work. They've worked for millions of others, and they can work for you, too.

You can master the art of self-motivation starting today. And in the process, you can stop being the kind of person who wishes for a better life and start being the kind of person who lives one. Are you ready to make a change? Do you have a dream that you feel strongly enough about that you're willing to try something different if it means you might reach it?

I hope so. And when you use the advice I've outlined in these pages to succeed, I hope you'll share your victory with me. Few things in life feel as good as knowing you've been able to help another person. So I hope you'll take a moment to email me through my website to let me know about your accomplishments, along with everything you learned along the way. Here's to you and your future… good luck, and know that I believe in you!

About the Author

Chris Luciano is an author and motivational speaker. Like his book, his presentations focus on scientific and verifiable ways to create personal change.

An experienced entrepreneur and hypnotist, Chris has a passion for understanding the inner workings of the subconscious mind and how the patterns we find within ourselves can either create or prevent success. His goal is to teach every reader and audience member how they can stay motivated, feel good about themselves, and better their own lives through goal attainment.

Away from the stage, Chris has an appetite for travel and adventure. When he's not working with corporate clients, you can find him on ski slopes, mountain ranges, and hiking trails around the world. He also serves as a youth coach and donates his time to several charitable organizations in and around Maryland.

Originally from Baltimore, Chris has been blessed with a wife and two children.

www.ingramcontent.com/pod-product-compliance
Lightning Source LLC
LaVergne TN
LVHW011243080426
835509LV00005B/612
9780692794517